John Curry

Observations on the Popery Laws

John Curry

Observations on the Popery Laws

ISBN/EAN: 9783743309609

Manufactured in Europe, USA, Canada, Australia, Japa

Cover: Foto ©ninafisch / pixelio.de

Manufactured and distributed by brebook publishing software
(www.brebook.com)

John Curry

Observations on the Popery Laws

OBSERVATIONS

ON THE

POPERY LAWS.

Vultis exemplo majorum augere rem Romanam, *victos in Civitatem accipiendo?* Materia crescendi per summam gloriam suppeditat. Certè id firmissimum longè imperium est, *quô obedientes gaudent.* Nostrum enim fuit efficere, ut omnium rerum vobis ad Consulendum *potestas esset* ; vestrum est decernere, *quod optimum vobis reique publicæ sit.*

L I V.

D U B L I N :

PRINTED BY T. EWING IN CAPEL-STREET.

M. D C C. L X X I.

[P R I C E, a British Sixpence.]

TO

HIS EXCELLENCY

GEORGE Lord Viſ. TOWNSHEND:

LORD LIEUTENANT GENERAL AND GENERAL
GOVERNOR OF IRELAND.

AND TO THE

LORDS SPIRITUAL AND TEMPORAL,

AND

C O M M O N S,

IN PARLIAMENT ASSEMBLED.

THESE

O B S E R V A T I O N S

ARE, WITH THE PROFOUNDEST SUBMISSION AND RESPECT

D E D I C A T E D

BY THE

A U T H O R.

OBSERVATIONS

ON THE

POPERY LAWS.

IN every Conſtitution, political, as well as natural, there are original ſprings and principles by which the œconomy of the whole is con-
ducted : ſome communicate vigour, and promiſe
longevity ; others, ſeemingly performing the func-
tions, and occaſionally promoting the purpoſes
of life, tend ultimately to its diſſolution. They
are the ſeveral components of a complicated ma-
chine, acting and acted upon alternately ; now
co-operating, now counter-working, as events
favour, or accidents affect their ſeveral powers.
Hence therefore, the great ſtrength of attention,
and the great exertion of ſkill, neceſſary to produce all the Good, and remedy every Evil which
ſuch a Conſtitution is capable of admitting. This
is properly the province of the Legiſlature in every
Country ; and particularly in our own, where power
becomes either a remote, or an immediate delega-
tion from the people, this taſk of managing the
ſprings, or correcting the deviations of the ma-

chine of Government, will be the more difficult. A free people muſt be humoured in the habits, and governed by the principles, good and bad, to which they have been long accuſtomed ; and changes even for the better ſhould be cautiouſly made, without giving any violent ſhock to their prejudices. In ſome caſes, certain diſorders muſt be left to themſelves, to work off noxious humours : it being more prudent to take their cure from the hand of time, than to precipitate remedies which never operate profitably, when they are adminiſtered unſeaſonably. In more hopeful caſes, however, this work of time may be ſafely anticipated ;. and *when it can,* heſitation would be imprudent, and delay pernicious. The lingering diſeaſe may fatigue, the growing hectic may alarm, the patient : and a *new* remedy will be adopted the ſooner, that the *old* contributed but little to the relief, and ſtill leſs to the recruit of nature, in any ſtage of the diſorder.

To apply theſe general obſervations to our own caſe, it ſhould be noticed, that after the reduction of the old Iriſh natives, on the commencement of the ſeventeenth century, our Conſtitution, then in its infancy, exhibited uncommon marks of vigour. That after ſuffering violent convulſions in the time of Charles I ; it ſoon recovered new ſtrength, and from a promiſing ſtate of youth immediately after the Reſtoration of Charles II, it arrived by quick approaches to maturity in the reign of William the third.

It fhould be remembered alfo, that foon after the demife of that great Monarch, this blooming face on our affairs was overcaft; a cloud refted upon it, thin in the beginning, but thickened by time. It came on gradually, and was fubmitted to as a *tranfient* inconvenience, which fpeculative zeal imagined, would be repaid by *lafting* future advantages. It confequently gave no alarm; and the flight put upon it was the greater, as it fell only on the weaker part of the nation : the labouring and more numerous, but at the fame time the moft odious of any, who profeffed a religion different from that of the eftablifhment. We waited a long time for the expected benefit, but it did not arrive; our languor encreafed, and for fome years paft it very naturally made its progrefs backward, from the inferior people, to the community in general; other caufes concurred of late in this retrograde progrefs, till (notwithftanding all the vigour of the adminiftration) it began to affect thofe members, who from their fituation in life, are the fartheft removed from public diftrefs of any kind. The caufe I have mentioned is a capital one, and in perpetual operation. Happily perhaps, for us, it can be eafily removed if ever we fet about it, or think ourfelves fafe in doing fo; it was laid in angry times, and in the fears of our anceftors that great evils impended over this nation from men recently difarmed, and who having loft the *power* of injuring us, yet retained the *inclination.* However juſt thoſe fears might be, they ſhould not, certainly, extend to any legal diſqualification on any ſet of men, to render us *durable* ſervice ; ſince their diſ-ability to ſuch ſervice muſt undoubtedly involve a *durable* evil : and ſince any ſtrength gained *by them* muſt be ſo much acquiſition in our favour, to be turned *againſt them* on an emergency. Our real ſtrength muſt ariſe from the ſoundneſs of our Conſtitution, and from the circulation of its benefits. Should the principal of thoſe benefits be forbid to the greater part of our labouring people, to the landholder, to the citizen, and to the yeoman ; the hand of induſtry is *actually* and *effectually* cramped, from no neceſſity on earth, but what is impoſed by our thinking that ſuch men hold principles to which themſelves ſeem to be ſtrangers : I mean principles inconſiſtent with the ſafety of our *civil* government. I ſhall prove in the ſequel, that what I inſinuate is no paradox ; hiſtory and ſtubborn facts ſhall be my guide. We may therefore deſiſt from charging the wiſer part among theſe men with *principles which they abhor* ; other Proteſtant ſtates have done ſo long ſince, and take their Catechiſm (ſuch as it is) from themſelves, not from others who would faſten a different one upon them. In fact, honeſt men enlightened by knowledge, can not profeſs *two* Religions : one for the public to *deceive* it, another for private conſcience to *deceive themſelves*. Such men may be orthodox in their civil faith, and when they are, they can not be the objects of any penal laws, detrimental to the public ; tho' were their numbers but fmall, the injury could not be great. *As a multitude,* their inconnection, their difability, their lazinefs, their defpondency, their beggary, muft not only weaken the whole community, but affect its very vitals. You make them mere birds of paffage : and by giving them no encouragement to improve, to drain, or to inclofe the lands you let them for a fhort time, and on rack rents, you prepare them for their flight, and injure yourfelf greatly. You neceffarily import the fubfiftance of the manufacturer, the artizan, and but too often of the greater part of the people, from diftant regions : and refign to foreign agriculture, the ftamina of public profperity !

In truth the little ftrength gained, the great weaknefs incurred by the indifcriminate operation of our penal laws, call aloud for alteratives ; nor fhould difguft to a *new* remedy, nor diffidence in the hand that offers it, nor fondnefs for an *old* prefcription, ineffectual for feventy years paft, prevail againft a *probable,* or even *poffible* change for the better ; fuch efpecially as can be attended neither with danger or hazard, and from whofe operation fome ufeful knowledge muft certainly be gained of the *weak* foundation or *real* folidity of our former judgments. Such an advantage is not to be lightly thrown away. A retrofpect to *caufes* which perhaps we miftook, and to *confe-quences* which we have long felt, may put a clue into our hands for guiding us to ufeful truths thro' the labyrinth of opinion, in which we have wandered but too long. It may also help to a solution of some questions very important to our true interests, in this happy repose for such an examination : In the first place, whether measures expedient in certain circumstances, might not be highly injurious to public prosperity, when such circumstances no longer exist, nor can possibly return ? Whether ill information had any share in disposing of our former determinations, relatively to the distribution of rewards and punishments ? And lastly, whether a succession of facts has *contradicted* or *justified* our judgments of men and things, since our deviation from the plan of policy established by K. WILLIAM III. for the prosperity of this kingdom ?

The means of happiness to any country are two-fold : drawn on the *one* hand from its *natural* advantages, on the *other* from the wisdom of its *political institutions* ; *either* may lay the foundation, nothing but the union and co-operation *of both* can erect the edifice of public prosperity. On such a rock ours has been built by the late King William, and if we have removed any of the pillars which supported that edifice, it is time, *in this day of leisure for it*, to replace them. That the present administration will lend a helping hand, we have no reason to doubt ; as indeed we have had repeated proofs of the best disposition towards this nation in every act of executive government, since the succession of the present

Royal Family took place. The natural advantages of this island are spread before us, not only with a liberal, but profuse hand. Surrounded on all sides with the most fruitful coasts; possessed of the safest harbours; happy in a moderate climate; happier still in the fecundity of our soil; peculiarly. advantaged by our situation between the old and new world. These are the bounties of Providence to this nation. *On the other hand*, our civil constitution settled on unshaken foundations soon after the Revolution in *eighty eight*; all party contentions about power, long since at an end. Property ascertained by *old laws*, guarded by *old prescription*, fortified by *every legal sanction*; frequent sessions of the legislature thro' a period of eighty years, *uninterrupted from foreign hostility or domestic rebellion*. A new improvement of the constitution by more frequent elections of our representatives in parliament; all parties revering the present establishment; united in loyalty to the same prince; steady in obedience to the same laws. These are the provisions which an excellent constitution, strengthened by length of time, has made for improving the advantages which our soil and situation intitle us to: and though all this be undeniably a fair representation, as far as I have deduced it; yet I am sensible how readily it might be rejected by a stranger of any curiosity, who should take a survey in person, of the present face of nature, and of. the condition of the people in this island. To what has been fo truly advanced in our favour, he would oppofe facts equally undeniable; the miferable appearance of the country after this repofe of eighty years, our fields uncultivated, our waftes unreclaimed, our labouring people deftitute of food and raiment; our roads and villages infefted by vagrant beggars; in *many* parts houfes abandoned: in *moft*, no houfes built, no improvements made. Numbers of our manufacturers yearly on the wing: others with what monied property they can acquire, flying for fecurity to foreign lands: ftill greater numbers, under the compulfion of *invincible diftrefs*, turning exiles in their own defence; and to complete all, public credit at the loweft ebb, and bankruptcies in every quarter of the kingdom! All this, fuch a traveller would oppofe to the reprefentation given above, and he would have no hefitation in pronouncing, that *in a country fo highly favoured by nature*, the inhabitants could not be miferable, *without fome defect in our laws.*

Whether any laws enacted within the prefent century, and ftill in force, are defective, or operated differently from the intention of the legiflature, may be well worthy of confideration. I enter into fuch a difquifition, with all the deference due to the wifdom of our reprefentatives, and with fome confidence, as I apply to men who cannot be deceived by mine, or any other writer's miftakes, relatively to the good of their country; but who, however, may want to be reminded, rather than informed, of the truths I unfold. To such men, enlightened by knowledge, and inftructed by experience, such an application as the prefent, fhould properly be made, as it must be *from them*, and *them alone*, that a redrefs of our prefent grievances can be obtained. I am alfo the more emboldened to offer the following hints, as moft of the arguments which run through this fhort tract, have been borrowed from as able men, and as eminent patriots, as the prefent age has produced.

The capital evils which were thus brought upon us *gradually*, from a *tolerable* to a *weak* ftate, and from *that* to our prefent exhaufted condition, cannot with juftice be imputed to any adminiftration ; and he who would charge them on the *prefent*, muft have but a poor alternative in his choice, between his real or pretended ignorance : they have arifen chiefly from two *principal* fources ; from our *wealthy* Gentry who defert this country, and from our *wafting* and *wafted* Papifts, who remain in it ; from thofe who eat their bread in foreign lands, and thofe who oblige us to eat the bread of foreign foils here at home ; in a word, from thofe who have *great landed property* in this ifland, and thofe who have *none*, except a precarious one, limited in duration, and circumfcribed in profit. Under fuch a wafte from foreign and domeftic caufes, this nation cannot thrive, but muft be undone inevitably, unlefs fome fpeedy remedy is applied. One part of the fubject is fo fully handled by an eminent lawyer, in his new *LIST OF ABSENTEES, and in his obferva- tions on the ftate of our commerce and manufac- tures in 1769, that nothing can be added to en- force his argument. To the *fecond*, I fhall en- deavour to fpeak with inferior abilities, yet with the *partiality* due to the good of my country, with the *impartiality* alfo due to truth, and with the *deference* due to the experience of all free nations. On fuch ground I run no hazard in meeting the good fenfe of men, too well guarded to be in- tangled in the fnares of controverfy, too know- ing not to reject ideas repugnant to the intereft of their country, and too wife not to adopt every *practicable* fcheme for its advantage.

It is a truth, I believe, univerfally agreed up- on, that the Papifts of this kingdom have for feventy years paft, been an infuperable obftacle to its profperity. Cut off from the principal be- nefits of its free conftitution, they *neceffarily* be- come a difeafe within its bowels ; acting *againft it*, from an incapacity to act *for it*. We need not hefitate, therefore, in pronouncing them *the worft* kind of fubjects, that can exift in a country which fubfifts *chiefly* by *commerce* and *ufeful arts*. The poffibility of rendering them *ufeful* fubjects, which with fome may ftill be a great queftion, was *none* to the late King WILLIAM, who proved his theory by his practice, and recommended *both*

* Dub. printed by G. Faulkner, 1769.

by his fuccefs. He was a prince of great knowledge, as well as experience, and his authority
fhould have great weight in deciding on fo important a point as this before us, wherein the *co-
operation* or *inactivity* of a million of people is concerned. He hated popery, no doubt, as far as a
prince of his enlarged principles could hate any
religion ; but he drove not his popifh fubjects into
a ftate of *political apathy*, much lefs into a ftate of
defpondency and *inconnexion*. *He proportioned civil
punifhment, to the extent and reality of the civil
crime*, and having divefted the religious diffenters,
moft hateful to his people, of any power *to injure* the new eftablifhment, *he ftopped there*, and
divefted them of none *to ftrengthen it*. It was
a ftrain of wifdom he learned in his native country ; a policy which operated invariably in *Holland*, fince a period was put to the filly religious
difputes which coft the virtuous *Barnevelt* his
life, and drove *Grotius*, the glory of that country, into exile.

King *William* it is well known, was obliged
to purfue fome meafures difagreeable to him ; His
indulgence to the Irifh Papifts *was not of the number* ; the affection which they bore to the only
monarch of the *Stuart race*, who could be faid to
favour them, produced very naturally their *aver-
fion* to him. They oppofed him in arms, and
they yielded *reluctantly* to his government. In
the meafure which followed, we find the vaft
difference between the feverity of *fpiritual animo-*

rity, and the mild chaſtiſement of *political juſtice*. That monarch was not content with conquering thoſe rebellious ſubjects in the field; he ſoon after conquered *their paſſions*. Inſtead of *meeting* the oppreſſion they *feared*, they *found* the protection they *wanted*. He only ſtripped them of what they were no way intitled to, civil and military preferments. He did not ſtrip them of *property*, *but confirmed it to them in the fulleſt extent*, with the power of acquiring more, *uncircumſcribed by penalties*, *unimpeached by mercenary informers*. Whatever honeſt induſtry could *procure*, they were legally qualified to *realize*. Their condition was happy, *becauſe it was bounded by ſecurity*; the condition of their Proteſtant brethren was ſtill *more* happy, *becauſe legiſlation*, *with every power civil*, *military and eccleſiaſtical*, *was put into their hands*. On ſuch foundations, as on a rock of adamant, did King *William* eſtabliſh the conſtitution; fortifying the power of the ſtate; ſecuring the natural rights of individuals! The Papiſts, like their brethren in *Holland*, co-operated *with* the public, and *for* the public, in their ſubordinate condition. They were inſtrumental in national proſperity, inſtead of being a heavy burthen *on it*; and they diſcharged a religious, as well as civil duty to government, *fortified on all ſides by the ties of intereſt*.

Such, I ſay, was the political conſtitution eſtabliſhed in this country by K. *William*. Why it was departed from immediately after that monarch's demife, and without the fmalleft provocation on the fide of the Papifts of thofe days, may feem unaccountable; that it was done on principles of found policy, may with good reafon be doubted, as the Proteftant intereft in this ifland was gaining ftrength every day, and *could acquire none*, moft certainly, from a perpetuity of pains and penalties on any religious Diffenters, whofe interefts were *on the fide of the civil conftitution*, and whofe conduct muft, in the general courfe of things, be under *the direction of thofe interefts*. Popery profcribed by law, hated by the public, depreffed by its own weaknefs, could injure public profperity in *no* degree, commenfurate with difability on its votaries, to enjoy durable property in land, or a fecure property *even in money*. It fhould feem therefore, that Q. *Anne's* penal laws, had their fource, not fo much in the fear of a remote and poffible danger, as in the refentment of former injuries, when Proteftants and Papifts (the two great parties on our ftage) contended about the mighty ftake of power and property. However natural our fears may be, or however juft our refentments; yet *neither* fhould hurry us out of the line of our true interefts. Refentment in public, as well as private life, is often neceffary and juftifiable. Degenerated into revenge, it becomes hurtful, by overacting its part, and may wound the hand that ftrikes, more than the patient who yields to the blow. That too much was allowed to this principle in our

own, as well as in other countries, cannot be
denied. It rankled, very naturally, in the breasts
of numbers soon after the late Revolution was
completed; and it operated with so much animo-
sity from the pulpit and press, that K. *William*
was obliged to interpose his authority, to silence
the clamours raised against the *articles of Limeric*,
before he had time to get those articles ratified in
parliament. And it must be acknowledged to
their honour, that some patriots, the most distin-
guished by their fortune and political abilities,
exerted a laudable emulation of the King's good
sense and equity, on that occasion. But fatally
for this nation, that great monarch's reign was
short. The fires he covered, and endeavoured
to extinguish, were soon kindled. The principle I have mentioned, collected fuel in abun-
dance, and the hereditary zeal of his immediate
successor (the last of the STUARTS) fanned
these fires into a flame, which without being
wasted itself, has wasted every thing that come
in its way, ever since.

We ought, undoubtedly, to persist in every
wise measure of our ancestors; but we have no
call, nor the least prospect of a call upon us, to
espouse their passions, or adopt their maxims, relatively to the distribution of rewards and punishments. Their passions had objects that do not
now exist; their maxims arose from the combina-
tion of both; and *all*, were the consequence of
recent injuries received from the partizans of the

late King *James*, and of the efforts of *France* to re-eftablifh that ill-advifed prince. In a word, their fears were, in a great degree, juftifiable from the dangers which threatened them from *abroad*, and from a diffidence of thofe *at home*, who were recently fubdued to the eftablifhed government. During his fhort reign, King *William* kept thofe paffions within proper bounds, as he was every day fetting bounds to the object which excited them. But that Monarch died; and the combuftible matter remained, getting great acceffion of ftrength from the claims of a Pretender to the throne, acknowledged by *France*, and fupported by her power. Thefe were the incitements to the penal laws againft Papifts on the commencement of Q. *Anne's* reign. Thefe objects of penal laws are all removed: in effect, we have no Pretender to the throne at prefent. *France* is weakened, and agitated with internal diftempers: and, in truth, had thofe dangers, which threatened our anceftors, exifted to this day, they fhould be far from being a motive to lay the profitable induftry, of *any* part of our people, under difcouragements.

The fecurity of any country, divided by religious fyftems, may be rendered *effectual*, by a legal toleration of all fects, and by a T E S T of fidelity to the civil government *from each*. To the prefent Bifhop of *Glocefter's* admirable reafonings on this head, nothing can be added, nor can any thing be objected, fave only, the gratuitous pofition, that *Papifts cannot be bound by any oath of allegiance to a Proteftant government.* King *William* thought otherwife, and the experience of our neighbours the *Dutch*, for near a hundred and fifty years paft, may enable us to drop fo groundlefs an opinion, for it is no more. Even our own hiftory affords abundant proofs of the refiftance of Papifts to papal difpenfations, notwithftanding the operation and feverity of Queen *Elizabeth*'s penal laws, to tempt them out of their allegiance. On this principle many of the old *Irifh* clans, and many of the popifh nobility of *Englifh* race, fought on the Queen's fide in the *Tyrone Rebellion*; and in *England*, when the nation was threatened with deftruction, from *Philip* the fecond's invincible Armada ; " fome gentlemen of that fect, (according to the profound hiftorian * Mr. *Hume)* " confcious that they could not expect any truft " or authority, entered themfelves voluntêers in " the fleet and army ; fome equipped fhips at " their own charge, and gave the command of " them to Proteftants : others were active in " animating their tenants and vaffals and neigh- " bours to the defence of their country. Such " was the loyalty of Englifh Papifts to a Protef- " tant Queen, and fuch their refiftance to a Pope, " who (according to the fame excellent writer) " fulminated a Bull of excommunication againft " her, had depofed her from the throne, and had

* Hiftory of England under the Houfe of Tudor. Vol. 3. Dub. Edit. p. 200, 201.

" abfolved her fubjects from their oaths of alle-
" giance."

In truth, there is not a Proteftant ftate on the
Continent of *Europe*, that will not furnifh us with
proofs of our miftakes on the queftion before us.
In the King of *Pruffia's* dominions, Papifts take
oaths of allegiance to that monarch ; no more is
required to enfure their fidelity ; and they are be-
lieved fincere, becaufe their fteady loyalty for
more than a hundred years paft, is a proof of their
fincerity. When the armies of *France* took poffeffion by force, of his late Majefty's Electoral
dominions, his Popifh fubjects were as faithful
to him as any other, and furnifhed a recent proof,
that perjury to a Proteftant prince, was no principle of their religion. Late as it is, let us, before it is too late, fhake off the fetters forged for
us, not by religion, but by the memory of former
animofities about power, in which religion bore
only a *fubfervient* and *fecondary* part. Let us not
deceive ourfelves, by arguments drawn from the
rebellions of Papifts formerly in this kingdom.
For three hundred years before the Reformation,
fuch rebellions were more frequent againft *a Popifh*
government, than fince that period againft *a Protef-*
tant government. They were evils arifing perpe-
tually from caufes which do not exift at prefent,
and indeed can never exift again ; from circumftances, wherein the fpirit of a fierce people was
irritated againft lawful authority, inftead of being
won to it, by any compofition with their *manners*,
or any prudent conceffions to their *prejudices*.

Political deviations muſt be common, where the lines of protection and obedience are but ill marked. The caſe is now altered : we know with preciſion, what road we are to take, and how far we are to go. The meaſures of obedience are well aſcertained, and every ſubject, Papiſt and Proteſtant, enjoys the protection due to him by law : but whether every Papiſt enjoys the immunities due to the public intereſt, and due to his merit alſo, is another queſtion ; tho' it ſhould be none, had we an aſſurance, that the old diſeaſe is cured, *or that the ſharp remedy is operating without an object*. To ſpeak without figure, the *reaſon* of every human law ſhould be tried by its *utility* ; and whenever that ceaſes, *the benefit* (according to * Judge *Lyttleton*, and to truth) *ceaſes alſo*.

The benefits attending a TOLERATION, and TEST of civil fidelity, will not be controverted, tho' the utility of overcharging ſuch a Teſt may ; for doubtleſs, the propoſitions in any Teſt, *ought not to go beyond their object*. For ſeventy years paſt we have propoſed legal teſts to Papiſts, which the majority among them have refuſed obſtinately, notwithſtanding the great benefits annexed to their acceptance of ſuch teſts ; and tho' their refuſal may be no proof of *the ſoundneſs of their underſtanding*, yet it is one, certainly, of *their ſincerity*. It is a proof alſo, that if they did not believe the

---

* Ceſſante ratione legis, ceſſat beneficium legis. Synopſis of Lord Coke's Commentaries upon Lyttleton, p. 95.

obligation of an oath *to be sacred*, they would not scruple giving us *duplicity* and *hypocrify* in exchange, for all the advantages of our free conftitution. The metaphyfics of any *eftablished* religion, fhould never be impofed upon diffenters *from it*; becaufe *civil* government being concerned only about their *civil* fidelity, a teft drawn from the principles of the religion they profefs, is *the moft proper for them*, indeed no other can be proper. Should Irifh Papifts, for inftance, fwear " all " civil obedience to be due only to his pre- " fent Majefty ; renounce the Pope's fupremacy " in Temporals, declare their conviction of the " incompotence of that Bifhop, to decide about " the civil affairs of any foreign ftate ; that he " hath no power to diffolve the allegiance due to " princes, or to difpenfe with any obligatory " oath to government," &c. Should their religion, I fay, intitle them to give us fuch a teft, no doubt, certainly, can be entertained of their *civil orthodoxy*. On the *other* hand, fhould any Papift refufe giving that teft, *a difcovery would immediately be made of his profeffing a religion incompatible with the fecurity of our civil government:* and his recufancy would juftify every legal feverity againft him. Men of fuch unconftitutional principles would, like buoys on the flood, point out our danger, inftead of leaving us under *any fufpenfe*, as at prefent, *about its reality*. Again, fhould the *greater* number of fuch fubjects, like their brethren in *Hanover* and *Holland*, comply with fo

neceffary a *teft*, we fhould *in that cafe*, be in poffeffion of a mighty advantage, *by having a line of
feparation drawn between our friends and enemies*.
We fhould know with precifion, the meafure to
be purfued in the juft difpenfation of rewards and
punifhments, inftead of *confounding thefe men in-
difcriminately*, as an incorrigible multitude, with
whom no compofition can be made, for the p of-
perity of this country.

Should, indeed, any fuch found members be
found (and they are worth feeking for) it would
feem, that they merit fome manumiffion, after
this *long quarantine* of political health, fince the
demife of King *William* ; and fhould any gentleman object, that their good conduct, fince the
promulgation of Queen *Anne's* penal laws, was
rather the tribute of fear to power, than the dif-
charge of a duty, which the Gofpel requires to
every government, fuch a gentleman has my con-
fent, as, I truft, I fhall have *his*, to differ a little
from him, and on furer ground. Indeed either
principle might have its fhare, in producing fo
good an effect, and it may · be hoped, that the
better principle, had the greateft. *Inability to
evil* is doubtlefs one of the ftrongeft fanctions of
government ; but *inability to good*, forms a great
weaknefs on its fide. " Penal laws (fays the Ba-
ron *Montefquieu*,) have ever an activity *to deftroy*,"
and they do it effectually, when the hand of induftry is bound up by legal interdicts. They
fhould not affect *guiltlefs men :* much lefs the

whole community, thro' their operation on individuals. Adminiftered in too ftrong a dofe, they fruftrate their own ends, and may create a *new* difeafe, without curing the *old*.

The old difeafe of this nation has been fo accurately delineated by a diftinguifhed * Writer, fuppofed to be a member of our own Houfe of Commons, that I cannot refift the pleafure of giving in his own words, the fubftance of what I have taken in detail. " Ireland is an ifland which may
" certainly boaft of natural advantages, but they
" have hitherto been unimproved, or unemployed ;
" with fine harbours, but little commerce, and a
" fruitful foil but little affifted as yet by cultivation.
" It contains about eleven millions of I.ifh plan-
" tation acres, not above two thirds of which
" are inhabited, and not one half under any rea-
" fonable degree of cultivation, which is evident
" from its never yet having been able to produce
" Corn, nearly equal to the confumption of a
" country, which has the feweft inhabitants,
" and thofe a people too, who confume lefs than
" any people perhaps in the world ; † taxed in a
" greater degree than *Britain*, with a great ma-
" jority of its inhabitants too miferable from their
" poverty, to contribute to the fupplies, and

* See confiderations on the dependencies of Great Britain. London printed for J. Almon ; and Dub. by J. Williams, 1769.

† See this fully proved in the excellent pamphlet from whence I take this quotation.

" above two thirds debarred by *religious* policy,
" from almoft every opportunity of contributing
" to the wealth or ftrength of the country ; who
" becaufe they are not fuppofed to be attached to
" the government *by principle*, are not to be bound
" to it *by intereft*; and by the evil conftruction
" of well defigned laws, are not fuffered to de-
" pofit with the State even *hoftages for their loyalty.*
" Who are not allowed either incitements to in-
" duftry, or pledges of fidelity ; by being pre-
" cluded from enjoying fecurity for their money,
" or any valuable poffeffion in their Land. Who
" are kept by the Laws in a ftate of preparation
" for revolt, without hazard, attachment, or ob-
" ligation to reftrain them ; in fhort without any
" intereft in the public prefervation." Such is
the delineation of this internal difeafe of Popery,
fketched out by a mafterly hand. We are deeply
interefted in its cure, and fhould it admit of
none in this Proteftant country, and *in this alone*,
we may fafely denominate it a felf-generated
monfter : the like of which, never appeared before, in the political fky !

Nil oriturum aliàs, nil ortum tale fatemur !

To be a little more ferious ; the infecurity
mentioned by this able writer, relating to land
and money, in a trading country is eafier to be
accounted for, than juftified by any principle of
found policy. A monied property, as life itfelf
(rifing and fetting in weaknefs) is of a tranfient

nature, and if not carefully tended, it will fly from us, when the lofs may be moft fatal, and leaft expected. Both muft find fecurity in the place of their birth, or be forced to find it in fome more falutary climate. For the credit of my country, I would willingly draw a veil over a fact, which in this particular diftinguifhes it from any other civilized nation. With us, there is no fecurity for money lent by Papifts, fave only, what may be obtained thro' the hazard of perfonal engagements; eafily eluded by family fettlements, or annihilated by the mortality of the borrowers. From fuch a precarious fecurity, inftances can be produced, of the ruin of many Popifh families in this kingdom. So deep a wound to the livelihood of individuals, as well as to public credit, induced fome worthy members of both houfes of Parliament, to provide a remedy; and from the time of the late Lord *Halifax*'s adminiftration here, to the end of the laft Seffion, Heads of a Bill were from time to time, brought into parliament for that purpofe : But fo ODIOUS, it feems, were the ill-fated people intended to be relieved by that Bill; or fo *crooked* did the object itfelf appear, (like a ftraight ftick between two mediums;) or fo flight was the evil, from the *apprehenfions of a greater*; that no effort of patriotifm, could hitherto obtain the paffing fuch a Bill into a law.

Deeply as the perfons concerned in the fate of that Bill, were afflicted with their hard fortune, thro' fo many trials ; yet to join my own fenfe, to that of feveral refpectable perfons, I do not think that its failure was any great difappoint- ment to the public. It was well intended, no doubt, but it feems to h..ve been clogged with fo many preventive and defenfive claufes, (as if the return of popery fhould be the confequence of giving expedition to the recovery of a Papift's money) that the fecurity intended, feemed to be fruftrated in a good degree, by the feveral rounds it muft take, before it could have its full effect.

Such complicated remedies may have their ufe in preferving the remains of life ; but they can have very little effect, in reftoring the vigour, or improving the complexion of a wafted Conftituti- on. It is not phyfic we now want, but fimple diet and wholefome food ; fome cordial to rev.ve us, not emetics to bring on new convulfions, while the old paroxifms come on but too frequently of themfelves. We have one fet of men to *reclaim*, and another to *reform :* Abfentees who drain the nation of its circulating fpecies, and Papifts who drain it of its people, and wafte its lands. To reclaim the greater part of *the former* will (we hope) be eafy to the legiflature, or at worft, they muft come back and refide among us, when their Tenants are ruined, and when little money can be found for exportation. To reform *the latter*, will not be difficult, when we fet about it in earneft ; unincumbered with ideas, which have no foundation, and apprehenfions of danger,·

which flew before King *William* fourscore years
ago, and had no exiftence *fince his time.* The
Papifts of this country have as little *the will* to
injure us, and if we pleafe, may have as much *the*
power to *ferve* us, as their brethren in the elec-
torates of *Hanover* and *Brandenburg* have, under
their refpective Sovereigns.

This *German policy* of uniting *all parties in one*
creed of political faith, gives fufficient fecurity to
civil government. If it doth not, I confefs, in
any *great* degree prevent the *growth of Popery,* yet
it prevents the *growth of inconnexion,* of *lazinefs,* of
inactivity, of *defpair,* and of *general poverty.* It prevents the wafte of lands, and the flight of unemployed labourers and manufacturers; and it prevents
the growth of popery itfelf, by giving an exclufion to
all its votaries from preferments ecclefiaftical or
civil. It was the happy policy introduced into
this kingdom by *King William,* as I repeated above,
and the good conduct it naturally produced
among the Papifts *of his time,* would not be lefs
operative *now,* at the end of eighty years, among
their great-grand-children.

By the penal laws eftablifhed here under Q.
Anne, the Papifts were put under a legal interdict, from enjoying any lands whatever (for it
extends, amazingly, to plots and houfes in corpo-
rate towns) fave only, under a fhort tenure : even
that, is made liable to a forfeiture in favour of
the firft Proteftant informer, fhould it exceed a
certain profit, prefcribed by the ftatute. The
operation of this interdict. in making fpies ex-

tremely vigilant, brought many suits into our
courts of law, and reduced many families to diftrefs and forrow. Yet this is but a flight inconvenience, compared to other confequences. It
has put a ftop to agriculture, and converted our
Popifh landholders, into a huge tribe of Graziers,
like our *Scythian* anceftors. Pafturage is *one* defence *with them* againft informers, and is their
fole occupation ; for induftry we cannot call it.
Careful however, of the true interefts of men reduced to the neceffity of leading fuch a life ; they
avoid improving, building, or inclofing, as well
to draw as much as poffible from an expiring tenure, as to prevent a temptation in Proteftants,
to take leafes in reverfion of the waftes they throw
about themfelves. Is this œconomy an advantage to *Ireland ?* No ; but it is a confpiracy, and
a licenfed confpiracy, againft its profperity.
Again, as thefe Graziers have no intereft in the
culture of land, they expel the poor labourers
into mountains, into towns, and into the neigh-
bouring kingdom ; fome to gain a livelihood by
thieving at home, others by earning abroad, the
rents of their plots and Potatoe-gardens, while
the wives and children of the greater part, infeft
every quarter of the Ifland, in the fhape of naked
beggars. This is no exaggerated account, and I
appeal to the knowledge of every country gentleman in the kingdom, for the general truth of
what I affert ; I appeal alfo to mankind, whether
this feries of evils, equally difgraceful and injuri-

ous to the nation, fhould be tolerated, on the fcore of men, who turn their farms into waftes, and derive all their advantages from encreafing their flocks, and thinning the human race? Thro' this paftoral employment, population meets great impediments, and one year of famine demolifhes almoft all that nature could produce in many; view here then, the unforefeen, but tragical means for preventing the growth of Popery: It is furely full time to put an end to fuch a calamity!

The tiller of the land, and the manufacturer, *are the two hinges,* on which the profperity of this kingdom muft turn: the one is the fupport of the other, and the credulity of a *future* age, will hardly extend to the belief, that any policy of the *prefent,* fhould make a feparation between them. To reftore agriculture, we fhould return to King *William's* principles and practice, by *encouragements to labour,* and *fecurity to the labourer:* to minds enlarged by knowledge, and inftructed by experience, this change of fyftem will not be difficult, and no danger can follow, while Papifts are kept difarmed *by law,* while (if we fhould credit themfelves) they are difarmed *by confcience;* while alfo, they are retained by *ftable* intereft, and (to complete our fecurity) while we have legiflation, and all the military, as well as civil power, of the kingdom in our hands.

For feveral years paft, we live moftly on the bread imported hither from foreign regions. We even import Corn from *North-America;* and we fuffer many of our people to tranfport themfelves thither, and for ever, to cultivate it for us. Here then is another expedient, tho' not fo effectual, as the returns of famine, *to prevent the growth of Popery.* For four years paft, this importation of Corn, has coft us annually, on an average, better than 300,000 *l.* which added to more than a million a year to Abfentees, and to other expenditures on articles of luxury or ufe, that we might either well want, or raife at home, has fo far exceeded all our profits on commerce, that we muft be abfolutely undone, without the fpeedy interpofition of the legiflature.

Let the bread of foreign lands feed our manufacturers ; you put the ufeful arts, and the moft ufeful of all, the Linen-Manufacture, into the hands of a ftep-dame. In the arms of fo unnatural a nurfe, the child muft be certainly ftinted : and until you reftore it to the true mother, it will not thrive : in three Provinces out of four, the richeft in their foil, and the moft convenient for foreign Markets, the Linen-Manufacture is ftill in its infancy : its progrefs is flow, and it will never arrive to any maturity, if you do not provide for its nurture *at home.* Whatever evil there may be in the growth of Popery, there can be none in the growth of ufeful artizans, or ufeful hufbandmen ; though the laws fhould punifh them on a religious account, they may however be loyal, and have the greateft inducement to be fo, from the lenity of the executive government, since the succession of the present Royal Family took place. In fact, they are not molested in the exercise of their spiritual duties ; and this, doubtlefs, is good policy, as well as great clemency towards men, guilty of no civil crime to juftify punifhment. Let us fpeak (it is time to fpeak) on this fubject as philofophers and politicians, not as Catechifts, who believe as they are taught, and who prefer a pleafing impreffion, to a difagreeable conviction. Magna Charta itfelf, annual elections of our Reprefentatives, and the great fanctions of the Britifh conftitution, were fought for, and obtained by our Popifh anceftors. If they did not fight in the caufe of liberty, and throw ramparts about it, we might be flaves, not freemen ; and an unweildy code of pains and penalties againft fuch of their pofterity in both kingdoms, as retained the religion *they* profeffed, feems to be a folecifm in politics ; unlefs the latter give proofs in our own days, that they are averfe to a ftill better civil conftitution, than their anceftors contended for. The oppofition given by Papifts to the Revolution in its firft progrefs, was natural ; on its becoming a *legal* eftablifhment, the wifer part fubmitted : the rebellion of fuch as continued in oppofition, was injuftifiable ; and they fuffered by executions, and forfeitures. The prefent generation are not accountable for the treafon of fuch men ; but follow the example of the wifer men I have mentioned ; they therefore merit fome reward, efpecially in a northern country, where every great national advantage muſt be obtained from the hand of labour, and hardly any, without the activity of that inſtrument. Let it not therefore be tied up, becauſe Papiſts rebelled here in times of a very different complection from the preſent. For evident it is, that under our preſent legal interdicts, agriculture cannot take place, and manufactures which ſhould be grafted on *that ſtock*, will produce but little, moſt certainly, when grafted on *any other*. A good *Agrarian law* will execute itſelf; it is not in the nature of things, *that any other*, *diſcouraging to the tiller*, can be effectual. Let this capital truth be for once admitted : let it be granted alſo, that agriculture, or in other words, the buſineſs of planting, building, and encloſing, as well as of tilling, ſhould be that of men, *ſecure from all danger in conducting it* ; not of men expoſed to great danger, *in attempting.it*. Popery is, at preſent, an incapacity, and juſtly ſo, to employments civil and military ; but it ſhould be none, as I have mentioned above, to any other employment, productive of general proſperity, and, conſequently, *of the Proteſtant intereſt* ; much leſs ſhould this Popery be ſuffered to remain an inanimate ſide in the body politic ; *clogging* the action, *damping* the ſpirit, and *affecting the very being*, of the ſound ſide, to which it is annexed.

By ſubſtituting imaginary to real danger, we often create, what ſhould not otherwiſe exiſt. The danger of Popery, or rather of Papiſts, was great formerly, when the Nation was divided into two parties, contending for power, and rendering their Religion fubfervient to their paffions. It was great, from the claims of the old *Irifh* to the eftates they recently forfeited by Rebellion : it was great alfo, from the fupport of powerful princes on the Continent, to the claimants. All thofe dangers from Popery, have been long fince extinguifhed ; and new dangers of another nature have fucceeded ; to fuch dangers, arifing from depopulation, and difcouragements to induftry, let us turn our attention. We can do fo with fuccefs : we have leifure for it : we have power and legiflation on our fide : we have property fecured by old poffeffion, and old prefcription : we are fafe, where our great-grand-fathers had every thing to fear ; and therefore fhould fuit our conduct, as they did theirs, to the nature of the danger which is moft preffing ; to the activity of a *prefent* evil, not to the unlikely contingency of a *remote* one.

The danger of Popery to the Proteftant intereft, was great formerly, from the caufes I have affigned. It is only great, at prefent, from the paftoral occupation of its votaries, from their inconnexion with us as fellow-citizens, from the infecurity of their poffeffions, *monied* or *landed*, from the miferable condition of the labouring people, and from the neceffity of emigration among great numbers, to procure abroad, what is refufed them at home. Such I fay is our danger from Popery, and it is great. Legiſlative wiſdom cannot put a ſlight upon it : and the remedy appears eaſy, on King *William*'s Plan, without perpetuating an unequal combat, between *the penalties of law*, and *the penalties of conſcience*.

Our penal laws, ſhould on the ſame plan, be ſuited, as I ſaid before, *to the reality and extent of the civil crime*, and this wiſe meaſure will be the more practicable, as the *civil crime* ariſing from *religious error*, can be eaſily detected. It is only putting the diſſenting Religioniſt, *to the teſt of his civil orthodoxy*, and this for more than a hundred and fifty years paſt, has been the proſperous policy, eſtabliſhed in *Holland*, in the electorate of *Hanover*, in that of. *Brandenburg*, and throughout higher and lower *Saxony*.

Theſe arguments, however unpopular, cannot be forborn, as they are highly favourable to the re-eſtabliſhment of the true intereſts of this country, in its preſent exhauſted ſtate ; nor is this the time for cowardice in politics, or for concealing the conviction, or renouncing the advantages, of any important truth, for no better reaſon, but becauſe it is odious to *unreflecting* men. To advance the Proteſtant intereſt, we ſhould avail ourſelves of every ſtrength it may gain, *from whatever hand it comes* ; and to comprehend it, in its fulleſt extent, *we ſhould ſtrip it of all unrelative ideas*. The Proteſtant intereſt in a *political* ſenſe (the only ſenſe in which our preſent ſubject is concerned) conſiſts in the *union* of the Proteſtant

powers of *Europe*, fo as to form a ftrength fufficient to preponderate the Popifh. In a *domeftic*
fenfe, it confifts in giving the law to our Popifh
fellow-fubjects, *in the manner*, and *on the terms*,
moft conducive to public utility. In a *party* fenfe,
it muft be confidered in the nature of a conqueft,
which when completed, includes the fecurity of
the conquered, not their deftruction ; the priva-
tion of every power *to do evil*, but of none *to do
good*, to the community. The Proteftant intereft
confifts alfo, in confirming to religious diffenters,
thofe civil privileges which annex them *to*
the civil government ; not in loading them with
reftraints which feparate them *from it*. The Proteftant intereft ftated on *fuch* principles, muft
profper ; *nor will it bear being eftablifhed on any
other*, but to its detriment ; in countries efpecially which depend upon commerce, and ufeful
arts : it cannot, doubtlefs, be promoted by de-
preffing a multitude of men, who fhould labour,
and want nothing but encouragement to begin,
and fecurity to proceed.

I am well aware, that the fcheme I have been
recommending all this time, *on King William's
plan* of policy, will be objected to ; as fuch a
fcheme would prolong the evils Queen *Anne's
penal laws* were calculated to remedy — a conti-
nuance of Popery in this ifland, and a fufpenfion
of the happinefs of becoming all *one Proteftant
people*. The reply to this objection is not difficult ; for it is obvious, that the extirpation of Po-

pery is not to be effected by thofe penal laws. The experience of feventy years fince their promulgation proves it ; and as thofe laws failed of the *good* intended, the *evil* attending their conftant operation fhould, as far as poffible, be removed. On the other hand ; if this political fcheme of King *William* is inadmiffible, 'till an identity of worfhip takes place in this kingdom ; there can be but one *effectual* remedy in fuch a cafe ; the cutting off at once, thofe cumberous branches which for feventy years paft, have retarded the growth, and wafted the fap of the only trunk, from whence we muft draw our political nutriment. However practicable fuch an amputation may be, it is not, certainly, in our prefent circumftances, eligible ; and if it be not, it were better to proceed on the model of our *Dutch Neighbours*, who have long fince fhaken off their captivity to temporary opinion, and adopted the permanent judgments of nature. They have facrificed their local paffions, and the ftrongeft of all, their *averfions* and *refentments*, to natural advantages : and inftead of cutting off thofe branches, *fo hurtful to us*, they have by care and culture, brought them to bear *falutary fruit*. In truth, to profelyte Papifts to our eftablifhed church, by playing the pains and penalties of *this* life, againft thofe of the *next*, is not the way to win the heart, or convince the underftanding. It is, I own, a way fuccefsful enough, with the rich and luxurious, who have old Patri-

monies to preserve, and very little religion to lose.
The pride of family, in such cases, is strong, and
and the worldly reward is great and immediate. Relatively to the industrious and inferior people, the
more numerous and useful part of the community,
such a scheme can never take place; because the human heart, *unprepared by religious indifference*, re-
volts against secular violence, active or negative:
and, certainly, when we punish men of this middle
station, for adhering to a mode of worship, which
includes persecution *in the number of its beatitudes*,
and outbids by future rewards the perishable gifts
held forth by the present life, we put them exactly
in the case of the poor traveller: the more the
fury of the storm laid claim to his cloak, the fast-
er was the hold he kept of it. Look over (in our
registry office) the list of converts made from Popery, in the course of these last seventy years, and see
what a mighty acquisition we have made! Were
the number tenfold, yet what proportion would it
bear to the number of Papists now living in seve-
ral single towns, not to mention the whole island?
and if the incentives to preserve antient patrimo-
nies, have *compelled so few to come in*, thro' so long
a period as seventy years; what prospect have we,
that seventy times seventy, without more effectual
means of conviction than punishment, will complete their conversion? Indeed, the hunger, the
nakedness, the wretchedness of the poor, the de-
cay of agriculture, and the quick returns of famine,
may well supply the insufficiency of penal laws;

they are at prefent the *preventive of preventives*, againft the growth of Popery: But as our humane legiflators, muft abhor its excifion by fuch means, we can entertain no doubt, of their providing a fpeedy remedy againft a calamity, which ultimately muft involve the ruin of the whole nation, as well as that of individuals.

The diftreffes of this country, particularly for feveral years paft, feem to have filled their meafure. Like an electrical fhock, they have pervaded the body of the people, from the interior part, who felt the firft ftroke, to thofe who were the moft diftant from it. The great demand for our exports, and the confequential flow of money, during the laft moft fuccefsful war, blinded us; and the blindnefs continued. We could not fee the ebb of this money-tide, on the conclufion of the peace, nor forfee the wretched artificial expedient of fupporting our credit, by the circulation of paper-bills. Lands rofe in their value to an unnatural height; they are now fallen, to the great detriment of the Proteftant landlord, who encreafed his expences, in proportion to the nominal improvement of his rental; and to the great detriment of the proteftant farmer, outbid by the Papift; who cannot fupport without fome tenure in land, and who generally purfues his paftoral life, rather for bare *fubfiftance* than for *profit*. Such evils, furely, ought not to be left to themfelves, for their cure. We know our diftemper, both in kind and degree. We have feen its effects thro' every ſtage ; and the remedy is eaſy from the preſent diſpoſition of the legiſlature, from our pre-ſent ſtate of repoſe, from the ſoundneſs of our con-ſtitution, from the good intentions of the execu-tive government, under the beſt of kings, from our natural advantages, and in fine, from the power of uniting the hearts and hands of all our people, to avail ourſelves, of almoſt every earthly happineſs, that God and nature intended for us.

About twenty years ago, ſome gentlemen of diſtinguiſhed merit with the public, propoſed to permit Papiſts to purchaſe our moraſſes and mountainous tracts ; as the converſion of thoſe nuiſances into profitable lands would adorn the face, as it would emprove the rental, of our iſland. Thro' ſuch a policy we could acquire *a great deal*, and loſe *nothing* ; it was beſides, an admirable ſcheme for employing our idle hands, and it would be a great additional ſtrength to ourſelves, to be turned immediately againſt the improvers of ſuch waſtes, ſhould they hereafter prove guilty of treachery or infidelity to government: But as the attention of the legiſlature, was *at the time*, drawn another way, that ſcheme was ſuſpended ; and we ſhould wonder, that it was never ſince adopted, had not experience taught us, that the beſt things are often little regarded, or abſolutely ſlighted, thro' the facility of obtaining them ; while thoſe of doubtful operation, are but too often preferred. In one caſe, there is no field open for the diſplay

of refinement ; in the other, the mind is put in
motion by difficulty ; is heated by oppofition,
and feduced by its fuccefs in the choice between al-
ternatives of uncertain benefit. From this conftitution in the mental frame, much good has been
omitted in this world, to fay no worfe. At prefent, we have reafon to hope, that no advantage to
this country will be overlooked, *becaufe it lies at
our feet : That* which I have juft mentioned, and
the INLAND NAVIGATION, are noble fchemes
for acquiring the activity and exerting the ftrength,
of which King *William* laid the foundation. No
objection lies againft them, and they are practicable. Indeed the fpirit of improvement has happily gone forth among us of late, beyond all former efforts. The DUBLIN SOCIETY led the
example, and rendered itfelf celebrated throughout *Europe,* by encouraging ufeful arts, and re-
warding the artifts, without any diftinction of religion or party. Many of its members have feats
in parliament, and will excite in others, the fpirit
infufed into themfelves. Enlightened men, who
love their country, know every danger to which
it lies expofed ; every internal advantage it is capable of improving, and every injury which former mifapprehenfions have entailed upon us. In
parliament, they will find men (many we hope)
actuated by their own feelings, and endowed with
the fame elevation of mind. Their combined in-
fluence will be great, while their proceedings will,
no doubt, be cautious. They will confider whe-

ther the prefent be the proper time for re-eftablifh-, ing the plan laid by K. *William* for the profperity of this· kingdom ; or whether the minds of the majority are prepared for it, by a nearer view of the confequences, which Q. *Anne's* penal laws have produced. The greater, and often honefteft, part of mankind, are averfe from refigning their firft impreffions of things : Be it truth or error, they are generally equally tenacious of the one and the other ; confirming by habit, but feldom try-ing by examination, what they take up fortui-toufly. Providence for wife purpofes, has given the human mind, this turn ; as truth, its object, could never be obtained in a maze of fcepticifm. It is, however, reafonable to doubt in many cafes : In political matters more efpecially, fub-ject to a thoufand accidents and fluctuations, a tenacity of opinion is, by no means, to be perpe-tuated, but varied as conjunctures and circumftan-ces vary : A wife man attending to fuch variati-ons, will hardly go aftray ; and to gentlemen who may ftill hefitate on the queftion of the fafety, rather than utility of King *William's* plan, or who may think that of Queen *Anne* lefs danger-ous, I fhall beg leave to fubmit to their confider-ation, the following queries from that great divine and philofopher, Dr. BERKLEY, the late bifhop of *Cloyne*. They are only a few out of the many, publifhed by him about forty years ago, for opening the minds of this nation, to its true and invariable interefts. The principles which run through thefe queries were my guide thro' the whole of the prefent work. They ftrengthen my argument all along, and fhould I be unfortunate in my manner of conducting it, I make the reader ample amends, by the following extracts from the * author himfelf.

QUERIES of the Bifhop of CLOYNE.

1. Whether a fcheme for the welfare of this kingdom fhould not take in the whole inhabitants ?

2. Whether it be not a vain attempt to project the flourifhing of our Proteftant gentry, exclufive of the bulk of the natives ?

3. Whether the great and general aim of the public, fhould not be, to employ the people ?

4. Whether there be any country in Chriftendom, more capable of emprovement than *Ireland* ?

5. Whether in fuch a foil as ours, if there was induftry, there could be want ?

6. Whether there be upon earth, any Chriftian or civilized people fo beggarly, wretched, and deftitute, as the common *Irifh* ?

7. Whether, neverthelefs, there is any other people, whofe wants may be more eafily fupplied from home ?

---

* See tracts relating to Ireland, by Dr. *Berkley* bifhop of *Cloyne*, republifhed by Mr. Faulkner, and to be found in his fhop.

8. Whether the public happineſs be not propoſed by the legiſlature, and whether ſuch happineſs doth not contain, that of individuals?

9. Whether we ſhould not caſt about by all
manner of means, to excite induſtry, and to re-
move whatever hinders it? and whether every one
ſhould not lend a helping hand?

10. Whether it be not a new ſpectacle under
the ſun, to behold in ſuch a climate, and ſuch a
ſoil, and under ſuch a gentle government, ſo many
roads untrodden, fields untilled, houſes deſolate,
and hands unemployed?

11. Whether there be any other nation poſſeſſed
of ſo much good land, and ſo many able hands to
work it, which yet is beholden for bread to foreign
countries?

12. Whether national wants ought not to be
the rule of trade? and whether the moſt preſſing
wants of the majority, ought not to be firſt con-
ſidered?

13. Whether it is poſſible the country ſhould
be well improved, while our beef is exported, and
our labourers live upon potatoes?

14. Whether the quantities of beef, butter, wool
and leather exported from this iſland, can be reck-
oned the ſuperfluities of a country, where there
are ſo many natives naked, and famiſhed?

15. Whether the way to make men induſtrious,
be not, to let them taſte the fruits of their induſtry? and whether the labouring ox ſhould be
muzzled?

16. Whether the public be more concerned in any thing, than the procreation of good citizens ?

17. Whether as industry increased, our manufactures would not flourish ? and as these flourished, whether better returns would not be made from estates to their landlords, both within and without the kingdom ?

18. Whether it is possible the state should not thrive, whereof the lower part were industrious, and the upper, wise ?

19. Whether we are not as far *before* other nations, with respect, to natural advantages, as we are *behind* them, with respect to arts and industry ?

20. Whether it would not be a poor and ill-judged project, to attempt to promote the good of the community, by invading the rights of one part thereof, or of one particular order of men ?

21. Whether there be not two general methods, whereby men become sharers in the national stock of wealth or power; industry and inheritance ? and whether it would be wise in a civil society, to lessen that share which is allotted to merit and industry ?

22. Whether there be a more wretched, and at the same time a more unpitied case, than for men *to make precedents, for their own undoing ?*

23. Whether any art or manufacture be so difficult as the making good laws ?

24. Whether an oath testifying allegiance to the king, and disclaiming the pope's authority in

temporals, may not be juftly required of the Ro-
man-Catholics? and whether in common pru-
dence or policy, any Prieft fhould be tolerated,
who refufeth to take it?

25. Whether there is any fuch thing as a body
of inhabitants in any Roman Catholic country
under the fun, that profefs an abfolute fubmiffion
to the Pope's orders, in matters of an indifferent
nature?. or that in fuch points, do not think it
their duty, to obey the civil government?

26. Whether there is any country in Chriftendom, either kingdom or republic, depending or
independent, free or enflaved, which may not af-
ford us an ufeful leffon?

26. Whether my countrymen are not readier
at finding excufes, than remedies?

28. Whether there be any people who have
more leifure to cultivate the arts of peace, and
ftudy the public weal?

29. Whether the wealth of a country will not
bear proportion to the fkill and induftry of its inhabitants?

30. Whether it is not a great point to know
what we wou'd be at? and whether whole ftates,
as well as private perfons, do not often fluctuate
for want of this knowledge?

31. Whether that which *employs and exerts* the
force of a community, *deferves not to be well confidered, and well underftood?*

32. Whether it be not a fad circumftance, to
live among lazy beggars? and whether, on the

other hand, it would not be delightful to live in a country, ſwarming like *China*, with buſy people?

33. Whether the main point be not to multiply and employ our people?

34. Whoſe fault is it, if *poor* Ireland, *ſtill continues poor?*

Ireland is *poor indeed*, though this long repoſe of eighty years intitled it to a better fate : the cauſes of this ſhameful poverty do not lie deep. They float upon the ſurface, and every party-intereſt (if any ſuch exiſts) nay, every *perſonal* intereſt from the great land proprietor, to the cottager, is concerned in their removal. If ſuch cauſes have been hitherto overlooked thro' inattention, or perhaps ſeen but partially, thro' reluctance to quit a profile view of things; now is the time for looking them full in the face, and of tracing back effects to their true fountains. Let the maxims which run through the above queries (from as great a man as this or the laſt age produced) ſtand before us as mirrors, to reflect realities; (our *common indiviſible intereſts:*) and let us lay aſide thoſe falſe glaſſes, which only repreſent the fears of *ſuperſtitious policy*, or the averſions of *ill-grounded prejudice.* I have endeavoured, for the good of my country, to explain a few only of thoſe cauſes, which have reduced it to its preſent exhauſted ſtate; and under the ſhelter of ſuch authorities, as thoſe of a *Berkley*, a *Swift*, a *Monteſquieu*, a *Hume*; I run no hazard of injuring truth, except by my manner of conveying it.

No detached obfervations from fuch men can be fo profitable, as the perufal of the whole feries of argument, in their own works. Therein we learn, " that in all free countries, the laws ought to be " framed on the *fpirit*, as the government ought " to be adminiftered on the *principle* of the confti- " tution." " That in cafes, where no legal dif- " tinction is made, between *real* and *problematical* " guilt, *public weaknefs*, muft bear an exact pro- " portion, to the innoxious *numbers weakened*." " That countries which ftand in need of induftry " require a mild and moderate government." and that, " Perpetuity of fervitude, is contrary to the " nature of things in all free ftates." Let fuch confiderations, with many more from the fame oracles, have their due weight, and engage us to reflect, whether the profpect of our *danger* from Papifts be in any degree commenfurate, with the profpect of our *fecurity?* This queftion fhould ftartle no man. Our *fecurity* muft arife from their co-operation, and from their having an intereft in co-operating: Our *danger* from ther inability to add to the common ftock of public profperity, and from their exclufion from the ftable profperity in the land of their birth. It fhould be confidered alfo, Whether we have not perfifted too long in meafures, which however excufable in our an- ceftors, are doubtlefs, at this diftance of time, no lines for us to be guided by? and, Whether any political fcheme, oppofed to the hearty co-ope- ration of half our people, can ever bring us to that

D

summit of happiness which our climate, our soil, and civil constitution intitle us to? And lastly, Whether it be possible, in the nature of things, that our penal laws against this people, can produce any other consequences for the time to come, than those they have constantly produced for seventy years past—misery to individuals; weakness to the public?

Let the voice of nature and experience be listened to: let men who were the organs *of both*, be attended to. * S w i f t who knew the interests of his native country well, and studied them long, assures us from his own intimate knowledge of the inhabitants of this isle, that the Papists, had as little *the inclination*, as they had *the power*, to attempt any active injury, against the present establishment: But that great genius shared the fate of other prophets, sent to notify impending evil. He was *not* listened to in his day. We the posterity, however, ought to avail ourselves of his predictions, lest the judgment we feel, should fall heavier upon us. Let us improve the dispositions of the children of those Papists he described, into an ability of being *useful*, not *inactive*, in the service of their country.

No Protestant nation on earth is more secure from any domestic danger than this, unless we create it, thro' mistakes, of which common men would be ashamed in the ordinary occurrences of

* See Swift's works 8vo. Faulkner's Edit. vol. 4. p. 367. and vol. 6. p. 110, 111.

life; or thro' groundlefs fears, that unhappy mala-
dy, for which we hope this great length of time,
has provided a fpecific. We form a part of a mighty empire, and as we live neareft the feat of it, we
are, in confequence, the moft fecure from any
danger foreign or domeftic, and likely from
caufes well known, to be the moft favoured by a fur-
ther extenfion of our commerce and manufactures:
Let us not lofe the benefit of this fituation, by
an exclufion of half our people, from a *fubordi-
nate fhare* in our *natural* advantages. Let us rather rouze them by encouragement, and take hoftages of their fidelity, through the medium of fecurity : means of all others the *moft powerful,*
and the *moft effectual.* We are not (and let us
thank Providence) in the cafe of a poor unguarded
ftate, fearful of a *wooden-horfe* from *without,* and
equally fo, of fellow-citizens *from within,* to open
our gates for him. We are fafe, where our anceftors were in danger ; and their remedy from
a change of circumftances, is become our difeafe.
View the policy of the *Dutch* commonwealth :
furrounded by a thoufand dangers from which
we are exempt ; they made their Popifh fubjects
their friends ; a part of their *barrier,* not againft
Popes (for Popes are no longer dangerous) but
againft mighty Popifh neighbours at their doors.
Their penal laws againft thofe diffenting fubjects,
are mild and precife : they are brief alfo, and
might be comprized within the compafs of a fheet
of paper, inftead of being-fwollen into fo huge a

code of *claufes, prohibitions, comminations, amerce-
ments,* and *interdicts,* as embarrafs the ableft
lawyers in difcovering the true conftruction ; and
fubject the unfortunate objects, of our own penal
laws in particular, to fuch uncertainties, as very
often to have no affurance, whether they are legally *innocent* or *criminal,* in many of .their ordinary dealings between man and man ! We furely
have more reafon than the States of *Holland,* to
reduce the penalties againft Papifts into ONE
act, of no great extent of pages. And we may
be induced to adopt fo wife a ftep the fooner, as
moft of the Britifh Colonies in *North-America,*
increafe their numbers and confequence every
day, on this *Dutch plan.* From the extremities
of the empire, they invite Irifh Papifts to a fettle-
ment among them, and they could never make
any acquifition of the kind, had they not granted
our emigrants, the fecurity denied them at home.
Thofe Colonies fucceed alfo, (on the principle
of fetting up manufactories) in carrying off numbers of our poorer Proteftant manufacturers, who,
indeed, cannot hold out, againft the dearnefs of
provifions in this country, where they fhould be,
and might be, cheaper than *in any other in Europe.*
" Shall fuch a mighty evil be tolerated ? fhall
" the remedy well known, and within our reach,
" be neglected ? and fhall we fufpend the power
" of mending our affairs, to exert a power, fa-
" vourable only to other nations to whom we
" owe no favour ?" Certain it is, that the fpirit

of emigration is never produced in any country, without great pangs, and ſtruggles, before it becomes prevalent. It never did, never will,· proceed from a ſpirit of wantonneſs ; and to make it take effect, you muſt depreſs your people by poverty, and wants of every kind. More improvements have been made in *North-America*, within theſe ninety years, than in *Ireland*, in the courſe of five hundred ; and it ſhould excite ſhame, as it muſt one day provoke indignation, to reflect, that ſo fine an Iſland as this, ſhould become a nurſery of labourers and manufacturers for that thriving Continent, as well as for other more contiguous countries : we want them at home : they will labour againſt us abroad.

No more need be ſaid on this affecting ſubject. Our ſtate bark ·is not now (as in former time) toſſed in a ſtorm, to juſtify throwing any of our goods over-board : but to be daily emptying it, *in a calm*, is ſuch a ſtrain of policy, as would aſtoniſh us, had we not inſtances of the like infatuation in modern times, and in other *European* countries.

THE END.